MUSIC FROM THE MOTION PICTURES

ISBN 978-1-4950-0239-7

7777 W. BLUEMOUND RD. P.O. BOX 13819 MILWAUKEE, WI 53213

In Australia Contact:
Hal Leonard Australia Pty. Ltd.
4 Lentara Court
Cheltenham, Victoria, 3192 Australia
Email: ausadmin@halleonard.com.au

Visit Hal Leonard Online at
www.halleonard.com

HOW TO TRAIN YOUR DRAGON

HOW TO TRAIN YOUR DRAGON 2

THIS IS BERK
from the Motion Picture HOW TO TRAIN YOUR DRAGON

By JOHN POWELL

Moderately fast, in 2

THE DOWNED DRAGON
from the Motion Picture HOW TO TRAIN YOUR DRAGON

By JOHN POWELL

Moderately fast

Moderately, expressively

Slightly faster, steadily

SEE YOU TOMORROW

from the Motion Picture HOW TO TRAIN YOUR DRAGON

By JOHN POWELL

Moderately fast, in 2

18

TEST DRIVE
from the Motion Picture HOW TO TRAIN YOUR DRAGON

By JOHN POWELL

Pedal ad lib. to end

ROMANTIC FLIGHT

from the Motion Picture HOW TO TRAIN YOUR DRAGON

By JOHN POWELL

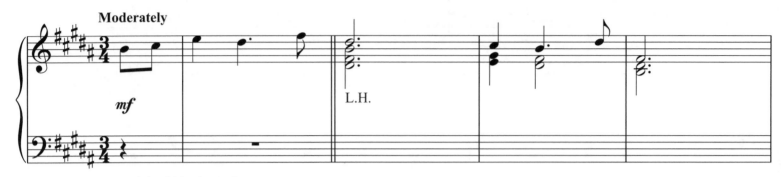

Pedal ad lib. throughout

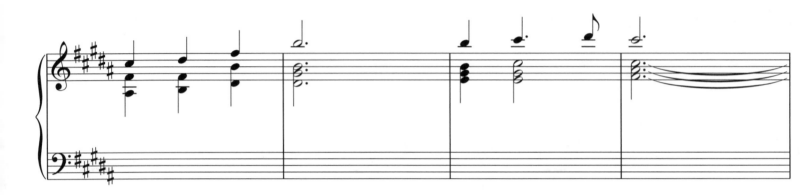

READY THE SHIPS

from the Motion Picture HOW TO TRAIN YOUR DRAGON

By JOHN POWELL

WHERE'S HICCUP?

from the Motion Picture HOW TO TRAIN YOUR DRAGON

By JOHN POWELL

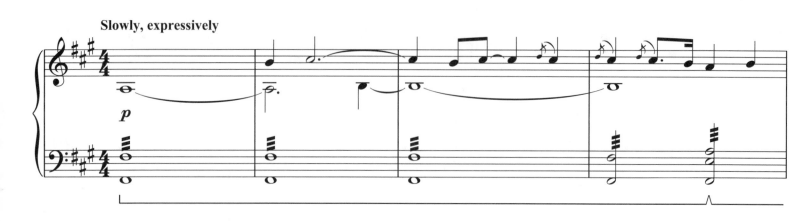

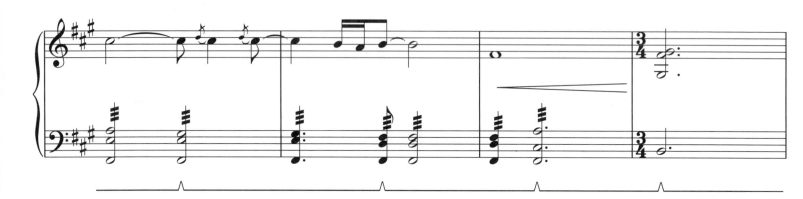

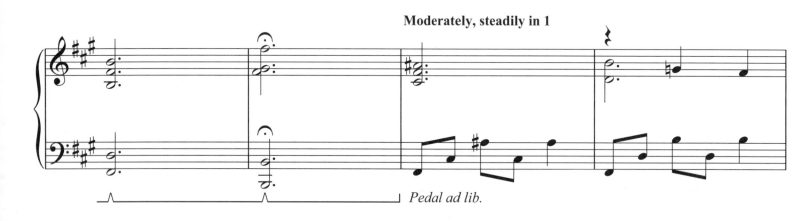

DRAGON RACING
from the Motion Picture HOW TO TRAIN YOUR DRAGON 2

By JOHN POWELL

Moderately fast

STICKS & STONES
from the Motion Picture HOW TO TRAIN YOUR DRAGON

By JON THOR BIRGISSON

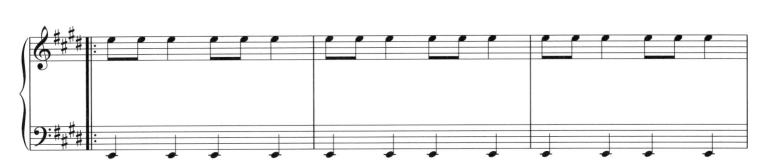

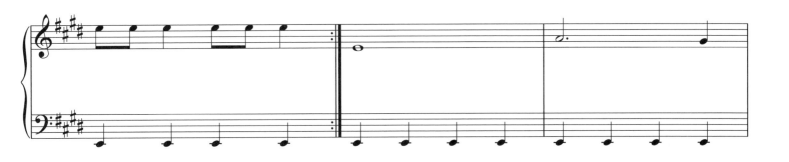

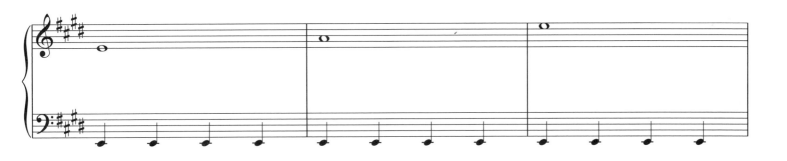

SHOULD I KNOW YOU?
from the Motion Picture HOW TO TRAIN YOUR DRAGON 2

By JOHN POWELL

Moderately, in 2

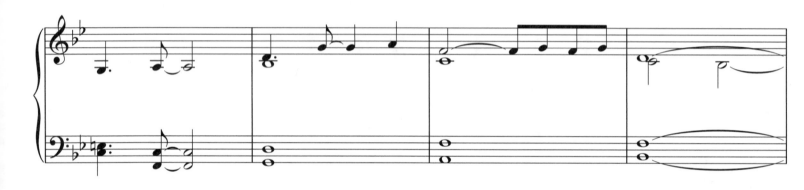

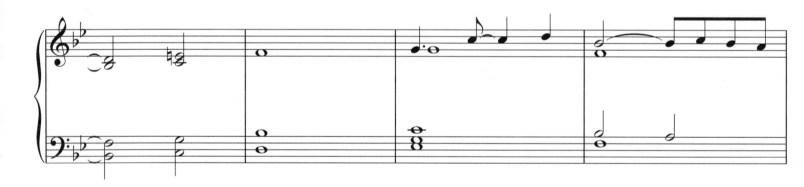

Moderately fast, in 2 (♩ = ♩.)

STOICK SAVES HICCUP
from the Motion Picture HOW TO TRAIN YOUR DRAGON 2

By JOHN POWELL

Moderately

Pedal ad lib. throughout

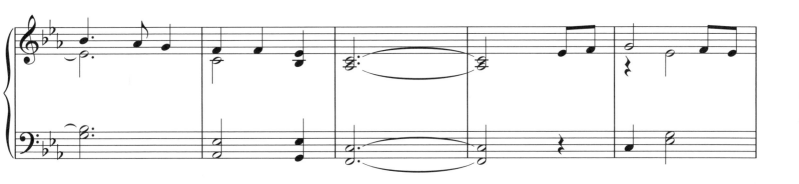

FLYING WITH MOTHER

from the Motion Picture HOW TO TRAIN YOUR DRAGON 2

By JOHN POWELL

Moderately fast, in 1

STOICK'S SHIP
from the Motion Picture HOW TO TRAIN YOUR DRAGON 2

By JOHN POWELL

WHERE NO ONE GOES

from the Motion Picture HOW TO TRAIN YOUR DRAGON 2

By JOHN POWELL
and JON BIRGISSON

Let the wind car-ry us to the clouds, hur-ry up, al-right.___

A - wake in the sky, we break up so high, al - right.

Let's make it a - round, let's